Koko-Love!
Conversations with a Signing Gorilla

by Dr. Francine Patterson
photographs by Dr. Ronald H. Cohn

DUTTON CHILDREN'S BOOKS · NEW YORK

Welcome, Dr. Patterson and
Koko! Is Koko aware that she's chatting
with thousands of people right now?
KOKO: Good hear.
PENNY: Koko is aware.

In loving memory of Barbara F. Hiller

Our heartfelt gratitude goes out to our dedicated staff and loyal friends and members for their continuing support. We would like to give special thanks to Karen Lotz, Amy Wick, Andrea Mosbacher, and Diane Giddis for their invaluable help in the preparation of this book. In no small measure, the efforts of Kevin Connelly, and Jody Weiner made this book possible. The assistance of Jane Abrams, Michael Grofe, Marilyn Matevia, and Dina Pettit is also gratefully acknowledged. Finally, we extend our thanks and love to three very fine animal gorillas: Koko, Michael, and Ndume.

And for all the children of all the great apes...that's you—*Koko-love!*

Published in the United States 1999 by Dutton Children's Books,
a division of Penguin Putnam Books for Young Readers
345 Hudson Street, New York, New York 10014

Printed in the United States. First edition. ISBN 0-525-46319-4
Designed by Leah Kalotay
10 9 8 7 6 5 4 3 2 1

koko.org

To bring interspecies communication to the public in order to save gorillas and inspire our children to create a better future for all species.

Guess Who's On-line?

Do you like to use the Internet?

If you have ever chatted on-line with a gorilla, you must have been talking to Koko! She is the only gorilla in the world who has her own computer. She is also the only gorilla who recognizes more than two thousand human words.

Koko speaks with her hands rather than her voice. She communicates with others by using her own version of American Sign Language, or ASL for short. Koko's human companions write down each word they see her sign. So far they have understood and counted more than one thousand different words in "Gorilla Sign Language" (GSL). Koko also knows many more spoken English words.

Koko lives in California with her adopted mom, Dr. Francine "Penny" Patterson. Recently Dr. Patterson helped Koko answer questions from fans during an on-line interview. Almost twenty thousand people logged on at once to ask questions or to "listen" to the famous talking gorilla. That's a record!

Koko signs "apple" next to her Apple computer. It has a special gorilla-friendly touch screen with word pictures and a sound speaker.

During the America Online interview, Penny took questions over the phone and repeated them to Koko, who signed back her replies.

Penny teaches the sign for "food," one of Koko's first words.

A New Mother for Hanabi-Ko

In 1972, Penny Patterson was a young graduate student, and Hanabi-Ko was a twenty-pound, one-year-old resident of the San Francisco Children's Zoo. When they met, Hanabi-Ko—or "Koko," for short—was living apart from the bigger gorillas. Normally she would have stayed with her mother for seven years or so, but she had been very ill, and her mother was not able to care for her. The University of San Francisco Medical Center team had saved Koko's life.

Penny knew that a chimpanzee named Washoe was learning sign language in Reno, Nevada. She wanted to know if Koko could learn to talk, too. Penny came to see

Koko every day so that the little gorilla would learn to trust her. She began teaching Koko just three words: "drink," "food," and "more." Each time Koko would eat, Penny would sign "food" and shape Koko's hand into the sign. One morning, Koko put her fingers to her mouth. She had signed "food" all by herself! This was a day to celebrate.

When Koko was three, she went straight to college. Actually, Penny got permission to bring Koko from the zoo to the Stanford University campus. There they could really concentrate on their language lessons. At first Koko kept signing "Go home." But soon she came to enjoy living

Koko's birth mother, Jacqueline

Koko, just a few months old, during her serious illness

Ready to roll

Do you remember your first word?

Penny, Koko, and Michael on the Stanford University campus. Koko signs "smile" to Michael.

in her turquoise trailer and working with Penny every day. She learned about "candy" and asking for a "tickle," and of course she learned about getting—and giving—a "hug."

Koko was acquiring words quickly. By the time she was five, she knew more than two hundred. That's just about the number of words a two-and-a-half-year-old human boy or girl knows. But soon Penny was curious about a new experiment. Koko had happily learned to sign back and forth with her "mom," and she

Hanabi-Ko means "fireworks child" in Japanese. Koko was born on the Fourth of July!

conversed with Ron Cohn, who took all the photos and videos. She also talked to the research assistants. Would she talk to another gorilla?

In September 1976, a three-and-a-half-year-old lowland gorilla named Michael moved in. After a little bit of getting used to her new brother, Koko welcomed him into her home. They had rough-and-tumble fun together during play dates. And as soon as Michael learned a few sign words, they began to talk to each other, just as Penny had hoped.

For a spoonful of food, Koko signs "eat."

Penny helps Koko sign "hear."

When Penny began the gorilla project, she wasn't sure how many sign words her adopted kids would learn. Penny eventually taught Koko more than one thousand words by making the signs herself, then helping Koko to form and repeat them, over and over. Penny would say the words aloud as she signed. She played games, invented rewards, and even tested Koko. She used reading lists and flash cards to see if Koko could learn to read.

The easiest words for Koko to remember at first were object words—the names of things, like "baby," "hat," and "key." Next she could understand verbs, or action words, such as "bite," "sleep," and "chase." (Young humans find it easiest to learn object and action words, too.)

Koko could use a few words about *when* something would happen, like "now" or "finished." She could answer many questions that began with *who* or *why*. In fact, sometimes she would answer the question but not tell the truth! Once she sat on the kitchen sink, and it fell down. When

Koko signs "flower."

Koko can recognize printed symbols and even a few words.

Penny asked her, "Did you do that?" Koko innocently pointed to the other human helper. "Kate there bad."

Sometimes Koko would play a trick. One night before bedtime, Penny asked her what color her blanket was. "Red," said Koko. But the blanket was white. Penny shook her head. "Koko, you know better." But Koko said, "Red, red, red." Finally Koko let Penny in on her joke. She laughed and pointed to a tiny piece of red lint on the white blanket.

Koko also learned how to ask questions. At fifteen months, she asked Penny to blow fog on the cold windowpane so that they could draw on it.

Because a gorilla thumb is smaller than a human's, Koko sometimes changes ASL gestures so that she can sign them more easily. Sometimes she also takes short-cuts, signing two words at once.

Michael weighs 450 pounds. He likes to have his belly button tickled.

Michael off for a ride with a friend

Majestic Michael

Koko became famous because she was the very first "talking" gorilla. She knows more words than Michael does, even now. But Michael started learning ASL at an older age than Koko did.

Even with a late start, Michael now uses more than five hundred GSL signs fluently, which means he performs them easily and skillfully. He is less chatty than Koko, but when he does talk, his words are carefully chosen and clearly formed. His

Michael enjoys listening to opera. His favorite singer is Luciano Pavarotti.

favorite food is a "nut sandwich." Think about his strong gorilla teeth the next time you bite into your peanut butter and jelly!

At times, Michael will fib a little, just like Koko. "Who ripped my jacket?" a volunteer asked. "Koko,"

Michael signing "nut." Gorillas have thirty-two teeth, just like humans.

Michael is a "silver-back," a mature male gorilla whose back fur has turned silvery gray.

Penny says Michael is the sensitive one.

the burly young gorilla replied. When the volunteer asked again, he said, "Penny." And finally, after the third question, came the truth: "Mike."

Michael is a very handsome gorilla. To Koko, though, he is just her little brother.

"Stink" can mean many things—it can mean "smell," "flower," or "stinker." Michael sometimes calls Koko a stinker.

Koko-Love

Koko loves Penny—then and now.

When Fred Rogers, the television-show host, visited Koko, he asked her his famous friendly question: "Won't you be my neighbor?" Koko replied, "Love you, visitor, Koko-love!"

On the back cover of this book, you can see a picture of Koko crossing her arms, with her right hand on her left shoulder and her left hand on her right side. That is one of Koko's shortcut signs, and it means "Koko-love."

What are a few of a gorilla's favorite things? We don't have to guess—she can tell us. Koko likes dolls and playing chase and stories and her family. She likes to draw and take pictures. One of her photographs, a self-portrait, made the cover of *National Geographic.* She likes to wear sunglasses and hats and she likes to eat.

Koko also loves Ron, whose glasses she likes to try on.

When Koko was a baby, she was afraid of her alligator toys. Now she likes to make them attack her dolls!

Koko does love candy—which to her means chewable vitamins. She even understands the word "andycay" in pig Latin!

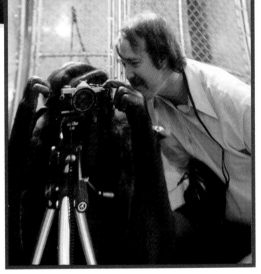

Ron taught Koko how to take pictures with his camera.

Penny: What do gorillas like to do most?

Koko: Gorilla love eat good.

Koko playing with her dress-up dolls

 Soft Good cat cat

Koko loved her pet cat, All-Ball, very much. He was a beautiful tabby kitten who had no tail, and that's how Koko named him. When All-Ball died suddenly, Koko was very sad. She cried in her room— *whoo-whoo, whoo-whoo.* (Gorillas cry only with sound and not with tears.) Even years later, when Penny talked to Koko about All-Ball's death, Koko had strong emotions.

"Remember when Ball died? How did you feel?"

"Cry sad frown."

Koko and Smoky

After All-Ball, Koko had a red kitten named Lips, and now she has a gray cat named Smoky. Smoky roams the grounds of the gorilla compound during the day or sleeps on the couch. When Penny is with Koko, Smoky can go in to visit her. Koko cares for Smoky as she would her own tiny gorilla baby, carrying her gently in her arms or on her back and never getting angry if she scratches or bites.

Koko's kitten basket

12

Koko and All-Ball

Ron's remarkable picture of Koko holding All-Ball made people around the world aware that gorillas are marvelous, gentle creatures who need protection themselves.

Michael prefers dogs to cats, because dogs are better at a good game of chase. He has a black Staffordshire terrier named Max. He also named Ron's female German shepherd Flower! Each morning Max and Flower wake Michael with friendly barking and a game.

Flower, above, and Max, left

The chase is on!

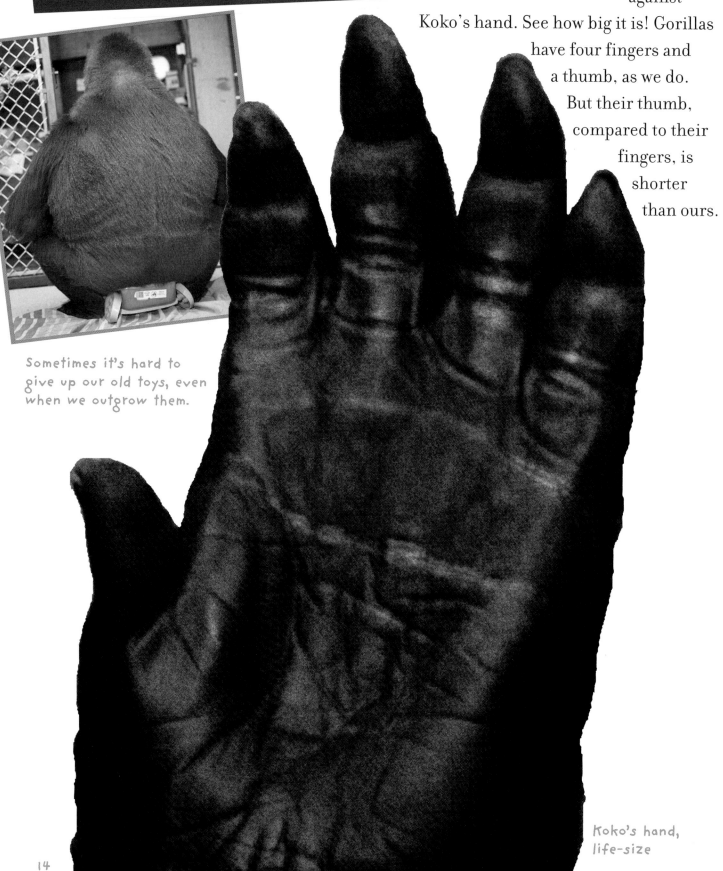

Just How Big Is a Gorilla?

Put your hand against Koko's hand. See how big it is! Gorillas have four fingers and a thumb, as we do. But their thumb, compared to their fingers, is shorter than ours.

Sometimes it's hard to give up our old toys, even when we outgrow them.

Koko's hand, life-size

14

Best of friends

Gorillas are the largest living primates, which is the family of mammals that includes monkeys, apes, and humans. A mature male gorilla can be taller than six feet and weigh up to five hundred pounds. His arms may stretch eight feet across, and he can have the strength of eight men!

Female gorillas are usually about half as large. (Koko's a little bigger; she weighs about three hundred pounds.) But when gorillas are born, they are even smaller than most human babies, weighing about four and a half pounds as newborns.

A gorilla's big toe also looks like a thumb.

Compare Penny's foot to Koko's.

MAMMAL CHECKLIST:
✓ Hairy bodies
✓ Moms make their own milk to feed their babies
✓ Flexible backbones

Koko had a basket of kittens—this is a basket of Koko!

15

Like You, Like Me, Like a Gorilla

As members of the primate family, humans and gorillas are very closely related. By talking to Koko, we get to peek inside the mind of a being very different than we are in some ways and not so different in others. When Koko goes to bed at night, she brushes her teeth, finds her stuffed toys, listens to a story, and says good night to Penny.

Here are two bedtime things Koko does that you might not do. Each night, gorillas make a soft new nest to sleep in. Koko makes hers out of blankets and toys, but if she were in the jungle, she would bend leafy branches to make a springy platform. Koko also sleeps twelve to fourteen hours a night and takes a nap in the afternoon. How many hours do you sleep? Probably not that many!

Koko signs "bad" when talking about her broken doll

Koko signs "cry" for the kittens who lost their mittens.

Sharing a laugh

Gorillas walk on all fours, touching the flats of their back feet and their front knuckles to the ground. If Koko were a mother, she would carry her baby on her back. So that's how she carries her kitten. And when Koko was a baby, that's how Penny carried her.

When Koko's caregiver, Joanne, was sick, Koko told her to drink orange juice. Your parents would say that to you!

Gorilla babies in their native habitat play games very similar to children's games: king of the mountain, follow-the-leader, and even catch, with a round piece of fruit. Koko and Michael play tug-of-war and hide-and-seek. But they wouldn't play catch with fruit—they'd eat it!

Gorilla Greetings, Games, and Good-byes

When Koko says hello to someone, she often likes to give them the "blow test," which is a gorilla greeting. When Koko appeared on *Mister Rogers' Neighborhood*, she blew a burst of sweet gorilla breath at Mister Rogers. He asked what she was doing. When he learned this was a standard gorilla greeting, he smiled and blew right back. Soon he and Koko were fast friends, and she helped him off with his sweater several times during the program.

Koko blows hello.

Mister Rogers says hello back.

When they like someone, gorillas can sit quietly and be very affectionate. Yet they also have a lot of energy stored up for play and even for confrontation. Gorillas tend to do more pretending than real threatening. They know how to "chest-slap" with their cupped, open palms to make a lot of noise. But usually gorillas don't really want to fight.

When Koko first met Michael, she was angry. (Sometimes when she is angry, she signs the word "red," just like a person who "sees red.") She decided to challenge Michael's arrival in her

Koko says good-bye— "Don't see you!"

Little Koko asks for a back scratch.

THE THREE RULES OF
GORILLA ETIQUETTE
Rule No. 1: Sit quietly.
Rule No. 2: Don't mess with children who aren't your own.
Rule No. 3: Munch on leaves.

house by chasing him. Soon, though, she realized he was not a threat. He was two years younger, and he was not going to be a serious problem for her. He might even be a friend. But as soon as she stopped charging him, Michael wanted to climb onto Koko's back and give her hugs. Now she had a new problem—too much love! So she hid under a washtub.

Maybe she was thinking, If I can't see him, he can't see me....

Come out, Koko, wherever you are!

What a Picture's Worth

Koko and Michael are both talented painters. Michael, in particular, has an amazing ability to capture with bright colors and shapes the image he is trying to portray. Look at Koko's beautiful painting of a bird and Michael's picture of his dog. Can you see what they saw when they were painting? Can you look through gorilla eyes?

Sometimes it's possible to have a conversation even without words.

Stink Gorilla More, a painting by Michael

Michael's portrait of his previous pet dog, Apple

Once Michael made a picture of a brown toy dinosaur with green spikes. First he painted the body with acrylic paints. Then he turned the paper upside down and let the colors spread. When he turned it right side up, he had a picture of a dinosaur with spikes!

Bird, a painting by Koko

Koko loves her blue jay friend.

Koko at her easel

What's That Word Again?

Koko likes to make up stories. Here is a story she invented with her human friend Mitzi Phillips.

Mitzi: Do you want me to tell you a story?

Koko: Good.

Mitzi: What do you want it to be about?

Koko: Alligator.

Mitzi: Okay. You help me. Once an alligator was very hungry. "I want ice cream," he said. "I'll go get some." On his way, he met a—*what*, Koko?

Koko: Bird.

Mitzi: "Do you want to come with me to get something to eat?" "Yes," said the bird, and the bird rode along on the alligator. Where did he ride, Koko?

Koko: Nose.

Mitzi: So off they went. Soon they met a—*what*, Koko?

Koko: Cat.

Mitzi: The cat said, "I am—" What was the cat? How did the cat feel, Koko?

Koko: Hungry.

Mitzi: When they got to the store, the man gave bird food to the bird and milk to the cat.

Koko: Milk Koko-love.

Have you ever tried to think of just the right word and not been able to do it? Sometimes when Koko can't think of the word she wants, she makes one up. It's gorilla poetry.

MATCH THE OBJECT TO KOKO'S NAME FOR IT:

ring	white tiger
Pinocchio doll	red corn drink
mask	elephant baby
ice-cream cone	finger bracelet
zebra	eye hat
pomegranate	my cold cup

Koko writes
left-handed.

Sometimes Michael can get creative with his
"spelling"—he's signing "know" for "no."

Sometimes Koko makes up words for things that even *we* don't have words for. What's that plastic thing that comes on a six-pack of soda? A bottle necklace!

Mitzi: So did the cat! And the alligator got all the ice cream he could eat.

Koko: No!

Mitzi: Yes! The alligator was happy.

Koko: No, sad.

Mitzi: You want the alligator to be sad?

Koko: Good, sad.

Mitzi: Okay. It's your story. So the ice-cream man said, "I don't give food to alligators! Go away." The alligator was now hungry and sad.

Koko: Sad, frown, cry, bad alligator.

Mitzi: But since he had been nice and had given his friends a ride to town, the cat gave him milk, and the bird gave him bird food. And how did the alligator feel?

Koko: Happy.

Mitzi: Yes.

Koko: Red eat bad.

Mitzi: Okay, you want more drama! So then the alligator went back to the store and said, "Now I'll have dessert." And he ate the ice-cream man!

Koko: Good visitor bad.

Mitzi: Did you like that story?

Koko: Koko-love good book.

The End

Koko and Ndume 4-EVer

Female gorillas mature when they are eight to ten years old. Koko told Penny she wanted a baby several years ago. She would point to a gorilla baby on television and say, "Want that." Penny hopes Koko will have a baby, because she would like Koko to be happy. Penny also would like to see whether Koko would make history once again by teaching her babies to sign GSL. Probably she would, because she even helps her gorilla baby dolls to form signs with their hands.

Ndume

It was easy to tell whom Koko liked and didn't like.

Koko's made-up sign for "Ndume"

So it was decided that Koko would get a mate. Unfortunately, there are not too many places Koko can meet eligible bachelor gorillas in person. So she did video dating. If she liked a gorilla, she would kiss the television screen. If she did not like a gorilla, she would click off the remote control.

One gorilla who Koko thought might be okay was a cute, big-eyed, black-back named Ndume. After some planning, Ndume came to live at Koko's compound. Now both have been living at the Gorilla Foundation

for several years, and they enjoy time together regularly.

Koko and Michael have learned how to have a conversation with humans on human terms. But Ndume, who knows only a handful of signs, also can communicate with humans—and with his two gorilla companions. When he wants food, he claps. When he knows he is going to get what he wants, he slaps one foot. When he has gotten it, he purrs.

Researchers have identified more than sixty signs in the natural vocabulary of gorillas, and they are sure that more gorilla "words" exist. Free-living gorillas also communicate with each other through body postures, facial expressions, sounds, drumming, and odors. Penny believes that Koko and Michael learned sign language easily because by nature they can use a complex system of gestures, just like their free-living relatives.

Koko and
Ndume play
hard to get.

The thinker

Fine Animal Gorilla

Koko gives a human baby a hug.

Dian Fossey, famous for her work with gorillas in Africa, gives Koko a hug.

Who is Koko? She is unique among her kind. She has acted as an ambassador for understanding between humans and gorillas. But she did not choose that job. It happened to her. We are very lucky that such a special individual was available for such a special job. Without Koko, millions of people might still think of "King Kong" when they think of a gorilla. Now instead they think "Koko" and see a beautiful, dark-haired being lovingly holding a gray kitten.

> Koko is aware that she is a gorilla; she calls herself a "fine animal gorilla."

And who does Koko think she is? She is aware that she is a gorilla; she calls herself a "fine animal gorilla." She enjoys looking at other gorillas on television and in books, and she plays with baby gorilla dolls. But maybe she doesn't think that being a gorilla is all that different from being human. Once she was given a stack of photos to sort into two piles, animals and people. Without hesitation, she placed her own picture right on top of Eleanor Roosevelt's the famous former First Lady!

Koko and Smoky kick back.

Koko likes to sign, play games, and make faces while watching herself in a mirror. At one time, scientists believed that only humans were capable of recognizing themselves in mirrors. Scientists now think Koko's ability to do so is extra proof of her intelligence. But Koko probably isn't thinking about this when she sees her reflection. She probably is just pleased to see such a "fine animal gorilla."

Koko makes a
face in the mirror.

Aloha for the Gorilla Foundation

The official name of Dr. Patterson's project—Koko's home and family—is the Gorilla Foundation (known on the Web as Koko.org). Located about thirty-five miles south of San Francisco, California, the Gorilla Foundation is a nonprofit organization that Penny and Ron started as a way to promote the preservation and protection of gorillas and other endangered species.

There are three kinds of gorillas living in Africa: western lowland gorillas, eastern lowland gorillas, and mountain gorillas. Mountain gorillas are so endangered that only about four hundred to six hundred are left on the planet. Western lowland gorillas, like Koko and Michael and most gorillas you see in zoos, also need help.

Luckily, a woman named Mary Cameron Sanford cares about gorillas. Through her company, Maui Land and Pineapple, she donated seventy acres of land on the island of Maui, Hawaii, for a new gorilla preserve to be built. The Allen G. Sanford Gorilla Preserve will be the only one of its kind outside Africa. If enough additional money is raised for its construction, Koko, Michael, and Ndume—and perhaps other gorillas needing a home—could move to Hawaii.

Where Koko lives now, in the Santa Cruz mountains, sometimes it is so cold the gorillas do not even want to go outside to play. Their bodies are designed for the heat of the tropics. On Maui, the gorillas will

Koko enjoys her Hawaiian lei.

enjoy a spacious sanctuary where they can roam freely in a more appropriate climate.

Hawaii also will be a more natural place for Koko to raise a family. In California, Koko and Ndume have not yet been able to mate. To have a baby, female gorillas usually need to be comfortable in their family group. Most family groups consist of one mature silverback, one young male, and three to four mature females as well as children. Koko has no female gorilla companionship, which may be why she has not had the confidence to start a family.

In addition to a twenty-four-hour research station, the Gorilla Foundation will build a Visitors' Center several miles away. Using modern technology, kids will be able to keep in touch with the progress of their gorilla friends and learn about how they can help gorilla conservation worldwide.

If you would like to help out at home or at school with Koko's move to Hawaii, you can write to Penny and Koko at The Gorilla Foundation, Box 620530, Woodside, California 94062

Don't forget to visit Koko's Web site at www.koko.org, especially the section just for kids. You can even join Koko's fan club on-line!

Give Me a Sign!

Koko (with a little help from Michael) shows you how to sign some of her favorite words.

EAT
Touch your mouth with your fingertips.

APPLE
Touch your fist to your cheek.

HUNGRY
Make a C shape with your hand and move it down your chest.

CANDY
Touch your index finger to your cheek and twist.

SAD
Move your open hands down your face while making a sad expression.

DRINK
Touch your mouth with the thumb of your closed hand.

TEETH
Point to your front teeth with your index finger.

KOKO
Keep your right hand open and touch your left shoulder.

SANDWICH
Cross your open hands in front of your mouth.

TIME
Touch the back of your wrist with your index finger.

BROWSE
"Browse" is what Koko calls her snack. Make a fist and touch your eyebrow with your knuckles.

LIP
This sign can also "woman." Koko sometimes uses it to mean "Penny." Rub your index finger back and forth over your lower lip.

UNATTENTION
Cover your face with your hands. Koko uses this sign when she doesn't want to pay attention or when she's not getting the attention she wants.

RED
Move your index finger down your closed lips.

VISIT
Touch your shoulders with your open hands.

Koko's Hands

Why do we talk to each other, humans or gorillas? We talk so that we learn, share, understand. We joke, laugh, comfort.

Koko speaks to us with her eyes and her fine gorilla sense of humor. She touches us with her warm heart and, most of all, through the way she communicates with her beautiful hands. But her future, and the future of other gorillas, depends on us humans to keep listening, to keep responding, and to keep speaking out against the destruction of the earth and all nature's wonderful creatures.

Now that you have shared this conversation with Penny and Koko, they're putting their trust in you to carry on the message. It's in *your* hands. **KOKO-LOVE!**